Eleanor Roosevelt

Eleanor Roosevelt
(1884–1962)

QUOTATIONS
OF
Eleanor Roosevelt

APPLEWOOD BOOKS
Carlisle, Massachusetts

Copyright © 2017 Applewood Books, Inc.

Collected and edited by Camille Arbogast

Thank you for purchasing an Applewood book. Applewood reprints America's lively classics— books from the past that are still of interest to modern readers. For a free copy of our current catalog, please write to Applewood Books, P.O. Box 27, Carlisle, MA 01741, or visit us at www.awb.com.

978-1-55709-059-1

10 9 8 7 6 5 4 3 2 1

MANUFACTURED IN THE UNITED STATES OF AMERICA
WITH AMERICAN-MADE MATERIALS

Eleanor Roosevelt

ANNA ELEANOR ROOSEVELT was born on October 11, 1884, into an upper-class New York family. After being orphaned at ten, she was raised by her maternal grandmother in Tivoli, New York. An aunt advocated for Roosevelt's education, and she spent three formative years at Marie Souvestre's Allenswood, a female academy outside of London.

She returned to New York for her debut in 1902. That year, she began a secret courtship with her cousin Franklin Delano Roosevelt. They married on March 17, 1905. Over the next ten years, she had six children. During this time, her husband commenced his political career, rising to assistant secretary of the Navy during the First World War.

In 1921, Franklin Roosevelt contracted polio, leaving him paralyzed from the waist down. While he struggled to regain movement, Eleanor kept her husband's political career alive, making public appearances on his behalf. In 1928, he was elected governor of New York.

Eleanor became First Lady when her husband was inaugurated as the president of the United States on March 4, 1933. She transformed the role from that of hostess to one of enthusiastic political participant. She was deeply engaged in the nation's well-being, continuing to visit places and champion causes that her husband could not. During the Second World War, she traveled internationally on the nation's behalf.

Her writing career blossomed during her twelve years as First Lady. Beginning on December 31, 1935, she wrote a regular newspaper column, "My Day," which ran for the rest of her life. *It Seems to Me* (1954) is a collection of her magazine columns. She also wrote innumerable lectures, radio broadcasts, and articles. Her three volumes of autobiographies, *This Is My Story* (1937), *This I Remember* (1949), and *On My Own* (1958), were later published in a single volume as *The Autobiography of Eleanor Roosevelt* (1961).

When her husband died in 1945, Eleanor continued her political service. President Truman appointed her to the United States delegation to the United Nations General Assembly. As the chairperson of the United Nations Commission on Human Rights, she helped draft the *Universal Declaration of Human Rights* (1948). She remained a respected voice in the Democratic Party. In 1956, she actively campaigned for candidate Adlai Stevenson. Val-Kill, her home in Hyde Park, New York, was the site of informal meetings with politicians including Nikita Khrushchev and John F. Kennedy.

In her final years, Eleanor Roosevelt published two books distilling her personal philosophy, *You Learn by Living* (1960) and *Tomorrow Is Now* (1963, posthumous). She died in New York City on November 7, 1962.

QUOTATIONS
OF
Eleanor Roosevelt

Quotations of Eleanor Roosevelt

Anyone who thinks must think of the next war as they would of suicide.
– National Conference on the Cause and Cure of War, January 24, 1934

Eleanor Roosevelt

I think, at a child's birth, if a mother could ask a fairy godmother to endow it with the most useful gift, that gift should be curiosity.
– "In Defense of Curiosity," *Saturday Evening Post*, August 24, 1935

Eleanor Roosevelt

A little simplification would be the first step toward rational living, I think.
– "My Day," Washington, District of Columbia, January 22, 1936

Quotations of Eleanor Roosevelt

I could never say in the morning, "I have a headache and cannot do thus and so." Headache or no headache, thus and so had to be done, and no time could be wasted.
– *This Is My Story*, 1937

Eleanor Roosevelt

*A*lways be on time. Never try to make personal engagements. Do as little talking as humanly possible. Never be disturbed by anything. Always do what you're told to do as quickly as possible. Remember to lean back in a parade so people can see your husband. Don't get too fat to ride three on a seat.... Get out of the way as quickly as possible as you're not needed.
– "Campaign Advice for Wives," *New York Times,* May 14, 1939

Quotations of Eleanor Roosevelt

One of our neighbors used to say that the only advantage of not being too good a housekeeper is that your guests are so pleased to feel how very much better they are.

– Preparing to host the king and queen of England, "My Day,"
   New York, New York, June 6, 1939

Eleanor Roosevelt

Will we ever learn to use reason instead of force in the world, and will people ever be wise enough to refuse to follow bad leaders or to take away the freedom of other people?

– "My Day," Hyde Park, New York, October 16, 1939

Quotations of Eleanor Roosevelt

The motivating force of the theory of a Democratic way of life is still a belief that as individuals we live cooperatively, and, to the best of our ability, serve the community in which we live, and that our own success, to be real, must contribute to the success of others.
– *The Moral Basis of Democracy*, 1940

Eleanor Roosevelt

We do not move forward by curtailing people's liberty because we are afraid of what they may do or say.
– "Fear Is the Enemy," *Nation,* February 10, 1940

Quotations of Eleanor Roosevelt

When life is too easy for us, we must beware or we may not be ready to meet the blows which sooner or later come to everyone, rich or poor.
– "My Day," Golden Beach, Florida, February 23, 1940

When all is said and done, and statesmen discuss the future of the world, the fact remains that the people fight these wars.
– "My Day," New York, May 9, 1940

Quotations of Eleanor Roosevelt

I have a great belief in spiritual force, but I think we have to realize that spiritual force alone has to have material force with it so long as we live in a material world. The two together make a strong combination.
– "My Day," Washington, District of Columbia, May 17, 1940

Eleanor Roosevelt

*S*ometimes I wonder if we shall ever grow up in our politics and say definite things which mean something, or whether we shall always go on using generalities to which everyone can subscribe, and which mean very little.
– "My Day," Hyde Park, New York, July 1, 1940

Quotations of Eleanor Roosevelt

Hate and force cannot be in just a part of the world without having an effect on the rest of it.
– "My Day," Hyde Park, New York, September 23, 1940

Somewhere along the line of development we discover what we really are, and then we make real decisions for which we are responsible. Make that decision primarily for yourself because you can never really live anyone else's life not even your child's. The influence you exert is through your own life and what you become yourself.
– Letter to Trude Lash, June 1941

Quotations of Eleanor Roosevelt

People grow through experience if they meet life honestly and courageously. This is how character is built.
– "My Day," Eastport, Maine, August 1, 1941

Eleanor Roosevelt

The battle for the individual rights of women is one of long standing and none of us should countenance anything which undermines it.
– "My Day," Hyde Park, New York, August 7, 1941

Eleanor Roosevelt

At all times, day by day, we have to continue fighting for freedom of religion, freedom of speech, and freedom from want—for these are things that must be gained in peace as well as in war.
– "My Day," Washington, District of Columbia, April 15, 1943

Quotations of Eleanor Roosevelt

One of the best ways of enslaving a people is to keep them from education and thus make it impossible for them to understand what is going on in the world as a whole.... The second way of enslaving a people is to suppress the sources of information, not only by burning books but by controlling all the other ways in which ideas are transmitted.

– "My Day," Washington, District of Columbia, May 11, 1943

Eleanor Roosevelt

The war for freedom will never really be won, because the price of freedom is constant vigilance over ourselves, over our governments.

– Speaking in observation of International Students Day, on the Columbia Broadcasting System's "Report to the Nation," November 16, 1943

Quotations of Eleanor Roosevelt

*D*o what you feel in your heart to be right—
for you'll be criticized, anyway. You'll be "damned
if you do, and damned if you don't."
– Interview with Dale Carnegie, *How to Stop Worrying and Start Living*, 1944

*I*n political life I have never felt that anything
really mattered but the satisfaction of knowing
that you stood for the things in which you
believed and had done the very best you could.
– "My Day," Hyde Park, New York, November 8, 1944

Quotations of Eleanor Roosevelt

*B*ecause if you know where to laugh and when to look upon things as too absurd to take seriously, the other person is ashamed to carry through even if he was serious about it.

– Letter to President Harry S. Truman, Hyde Park, New York, May 14, 1945

Eleanor Roosevelt

I'm so glad I never *feel* important, it does complicate life!

– Diary, January 16, 1946

Eleanor Roosevelt

*W*hen will our consciences grow so tender that we will act to prevent human misery rather than avenge it?

– "My Day," Berlin, Germany, February 16, 1946

Quotations of Eleanor Roosevelt

Have convictions. Be friendly. Stick to your beliefs as they stick to theirs. Work as hard as they do.

– On how to get along with the Soviets, *New York Times*, February 16, 1946

It is not fair to ask of others what you are not willing to do yourself.

– "My Day," Hyde Park, New York, June 15, 1946

I used to tell my husband that, if he could make *me* understand something, it would be clear to all the other people in the country.

– "My Day," New York, February 12, 1947

Quotations of Eleanor Roosevelt

*I*n our country we must trust the people to hear and see both the good and the bad and to choose the good.

– "My Day," New York, October 29, 1947

Eleanor Roosevelt

I cannot believe that war is the best solution. No one won the last war, and no one will win the next war.

– Letter to President Harry S. Truman, Hyde Park, New York, March 22, 1948

Eleanor Roosevelt

*F*or it isn't enough to talk about peace. One must believe in it. And it isn't enough to believe in it. One must work at it.

– Voice of America broadcast, Paris, France, November 16, 1951

Quotations of Eleanor Roosevelt

*T*oo often the great decisions are originated and given form in bodies made up wholly of men, or so completely dominated by them that whatever of special value women have to offer is shunted aside without expression.

– "U.N. Deliberations on Draft Convention on the Political Rights of Women," *Department of State Bulletin,* December 31, 1951

I have spent many years of my life in opposition, and I rather like the role.

– Letter to Bernard Baruch, November 18, 1952

Quotations of Eleanor Roosevelt

Where, after all, do universal human rights begin? In small places, close to home—so close and so small that they cannot be seen on any map of the world. Yet they *are* the world of the individual person: The neighborhood he lives in; the school or college he attends; the factory, farm or office where he works. Such are the places where every man, woman and child seeks equal justice, equal opportunity, equal dignity without discrimination. Unless these rights have meaning there, they have little meaning anywhere. Without concerted citizen action to uphold them close to home, we shall look in vain for progress in the larger world.

– "Where Do Human Rights Begin?" Remarks at the United Nations, New York, March 27, 1953

Quotations of Eleanor Roosevelt

A mature person is one who does not think only in absolutes, who is able to be objective even when deeply stirred emotionally, who has learned that there is both good and bad in all people and in all things, and who walks humbly and deals charitably with the circumstances of life, knowing that in this world no one is all-knowing and therefore all of us need both love and charity.
– *It Seems to Me*, 1954

*T*his is a time for action—not for war, but for mobilization of every bit of peace machinery. It is also a time for facing the fact that you cannot use a weapon, even though it is the weapon that gives you greater strength than other nations, if it is so destructive that it practically wipes out large areas of land and great numbers of innocent people.
– "My Day," New York, April 16, 1954

As for accomplishments, I just did what I had to do as things came along.
– *New York Herald Tribune*, October 8, 1954

Eleanor Roosevelt

You can't move so fast that you try to change the mores faster than people can accept it. That doesn't mean you do nothing, but it means that you do the things that need to be done according to priority now.

– Speaking in support of presidential nominee Adlai Stevenson's stance on civil rights, press conference before the Democratic National Convention, Chicago Conrad Hilton Hotel, August 12, 1956

Quotations of Eleanor Roosevelt

I believe that anyone can conquer fear by doing the things he fears to do, provided he keeps doing them until he gets a record of successful experience behind him.
– *Dale Carnegie's Scrapbook*, 1959

Eleanor Roosevelt

*A*nd the purpose of life, after all, is to live it, to taste experience to the utmost, to reach out eagerly and without fear for newer and richer experience.
– Foreword, *You Learn by Living*, Hyde Park, New York, January 1960

Quotations of Eleanor Roosevelt

*I*n the long run, we shape our lives and we shape ourselves. The process never ends until we die. And the choices we make are ultimately our own responsibility.

– Foreword, *You Learn by Living*, Hyde Park, New York, January 1960

*O*ne thing life has taught me: if you are interested, you never have to look for new interests. They come to you…. And there's one strange thing: when you are genuinely interested in one thing, it will always lead to something else.

– *You Learn by Living*, 1960

Quotations of Eleanor Roosevelt

The encouraging thing is that every time you meet a situation, though you may think at the time it is an impossibility and you go through the tortures of the damned, once you have met it and lived through it you find that forever after you are freer than you ever were before.
– *You Learn by Living*, 1960

Eleanor Roosevelt

You gain strength, courage and confidence by every experience in which you really stop to look fear in the face.... *You must do the thing which you think you cannot do.*
– *You Learn by Living*, 1960

Courage is more exhilarating than fear and in the long run it is easier.
– *You Learn by Living*, 1960

Happiness is not a goal, it is a by-product.
– *You Learn by Living*, 1960

Remember always that you not only have the right to be an individual; you have an obligation to be one.
– *You Learn by Living*, 1960

Quotations of Eleanor Roosevelt

*F*or freedom makes a huge requirement of every human being. With freedom comes responsibility. For the person who is unwilling to grow up, the person who does not want to carry his own weight, this is a frightening prospect.
– *You Learn by Living*, 1960

*N*o man is defeated without until he has first been defeated within.
– *You Learn by Living*, 1960

*W*hen you cease to make a contribution you begin to die.
– Letter to Mr. Horne, February 19, 1960

We have to face the fact that either all of us are going to die together or we are going to learn to live together and if we live together we have to talk.

– On why she invited Nikita Khrushchev to tea, remarks at a benefit for the Wiltwyck School for Underprivileged Boys, October 14, 1960

Life was meant to be lived, and curiosity must be kept alive. One must never, for whatever reason, turn his back on life.

– Preface, *The Autobiography of Eleanor Roosevelt*, Hyde Park, New York, December 1960

Quotations of Eleanor Roosevelt

I think I must have a good deal of my Uncle Theodore in me because I enjoy a good fight and I could not, at any age, really be contented to take my place in a warm corner by the fireside and simply look on.
– *The Autobiography of Eleanor Roosevelt*, 1961

We should begin in our own environment and in our own community as far as possible to build a peace-loving attitude and learn to discipline ourselves to accept, in the small things of our lives, mediation and arbitration. As individuals, there is little that any of us can do to prevent an accidental use of bombs in the hands of those who already have them. We can register, however, with our government a firm protest against granting the knowledge and the use of these weapons to those who do not now have them.
– "My Day," New York, December 20, 1961

Quotations of Eleanor Roosevelt

There is a widespread understanding among the people of this nation, and probably among the people of the world, that there is no safety except through the prevention of war.
– "My Day," New York, December 20, 1961

There never has been security. No man has ever known what he would meet around the next corner; if life were predictable it would cease to be life, and be without flavor.
– *Tomorrow Is Now*, 1963

Quotations of Eleanor Roosevelt

We must know what we think and speak out, even at the risk of unpopularity. In the final analysis, a democratic government represents the sum total of the courage and the integrity of its individuals. It cannot be better than they are.... In the long run there is no more liberating, no more exhilarating experience than to determine one's position, state it bravely and then act boldly.
– *Tomorrow Is Now*, 1963

What you don't do can be a destructive force.
– *Tomorrow Is Now*, 1963

Long ago, there was a noble word, *liberal*, which derives from the word *free*.... We must cherish and honor the word *free* or it will cease to apply to us.
– *Tomorrow Is Now*, 1963

Eleanor Roosevelt